This Dessert Recipes Book is the ultimate guide for anyone who loves to make delicious desserts. From cakes and cookies to pies, ice cream and more, this book has something for everyone. Featuring classic favorites as well as unique recipes from around the world, this cookbook will help you create desserts that are sure to please your family and friends. With easy-to-follow instructions and delicious results, these recipes are sure to be both tasty and fast. Enjoy the deliciousness of homemade desserts with this Dessert Recipes Book!

Dark Chocolate Mousse With Salted Caramel

Ingredients

For the salted caramel sauce

100g/3½oz granulated sugar
2 tbsp golden syrup
30g/1oz unsalted butter
80ml/2¾fl oz double cream
½ tsp sea salt

For the mousse

330g/11½oz dark chocolate (55-70% cocoa solids), chopped into small pieces
30g/1oz unsalted butter
8 free-range eggs, separated
1 tbsp caster sugar
whipped double cream, to serve

For the Salted Caramel Sauce:

In a heavy-bottomed saucepan, heat the granulated sugar and golden syrup over low heat until the sugar has melted and the mixture turns a deep golden color.

Add the unsalted butter to the pan and stir until it has melted and mixed in with the sugar mixture.

Remove the pan from the heat and slowly pour in the double cream while stirring constantly.

Add the sea salt and stir until the sauce is smooth.

Set aside the salted caramel sauce to cool while you prepare the mousse.

For the Dark Chocolate Mousse:

In a heatproof bowl set over a pan of simmering water, melt the chopped dark chocolate and unsalted butter, stirring occasionally until the mixture is smooth and fully melted.

Remove the bowl from the heat and allow it to cool slightly.

In a separate bowl, beat the egg whites until they form stiff peaks.

In another bowl, beat the egg yolks and caster sugar until the mixture is pale and fluffy.

Fold the melted chocolate mixture into the egg yolk mixture, and then fold in the beaten egg whites until the mixture is smooth and fully combined.

Pour the chocolate mousse mixture into serving dishes and chill in the refrigerator for at least two hours, or until set.

Serve the chilled chocolate mousse with a drizzle of the salted caramel sauce and a dollop of whipped double cream. Enjoy!

Pecan Chocolate Bread Pudding

Recipe for Pecan Chocolate Bread Pudding:

Ingredients:

550g thick-sliced white bread, crusts removed
Unsalted butter, at room temperature
6 eggs, lightly beaten
60g caster sugar
2 tsp cocoa, sifted, plus extra to serve
140g dark (70%) chocolate buttons
300ml pure (thin) cream
1 tsp vanilla bean paste
100g pecans, roughly chopped

Instructions:

Preheat the oven to 180C/350F.

Butter a 25cm x 18cm ovenproof dish.

Cut the bread into 2cm cubes and place them in the buttered dish.

In a large mixing bowl, whisk the eggs, caster sugar, and cocoa together until well combined.

Melt the chocolate buttons in a heatproof bowl set over a pan of simmering water, stirring until smooth.

Add the melted chocolate to the egg mixture, stirring until well combined.

Add the cream and vanilla bean paste to the mixture, whisking until well combined.

Pour the mixture over the bread cubes, stirring until the bread is fully coated.

Sprinkle the chopped pecans over the top of the mixture.

Bake in the preheated oven for 35-40 minutes, or until the bread pudding is golden brown and set.

Remove the bread pudding from the oven and allow it to cool for a few minutes.

Sprinkle some extra cocoa over the top of the bread pudding and serve warm.

Enjoy your delicious Pecan Chocolate Bread Pudding!

Blueberry Lemon Vanilla Tart

Ingredients

3 cups Fresh Blueberries.
2 tablespoons Cornstarch.
1/4 cup Honey.
1 tablespoon Lemon Zest.
1 teaspoon Lemon Juice.
1 tablespoon Fresh Thyme.
1 teaspoon Vanilla Extract.
1 sheet Puff Pastry thawed, cut into four rectangles.

To make the blueberry filling, combine the fresh blueberries, cornstarch, honey, lemon zest, lemon juice, thyme and vanilla extract in a medium saucepan. Cook over medium heat for about 10 minutes, stirring occasionally until thickened. Remove from heat and cool slightly.

Preheat your oven to 400°F (204°C). Line a baking sheet with parchment paper.

Place the four puff pastry rectangles on the baking sheet and spoon approximately 1/4 cup of the blueberry mixture onto each rectangle. Spread it out to within about an inch of the edges. Sprinkle lightly with sugar if desired.

Bake in preheated oven for 20 minutes or until golden brown. Remove from oven and cool before serving. Enjoy!

Serve with a dollop of whipped cream or ice cream, if desired. Enjoy!

Cherry Strawberry Pie

Ingredients
frozen or fresh sweet cherries (sour cherries can be used but see the note to make the necessary swaps to the recipe)
strawberries.
granulated sugar.
cream cheese (this can be replaced with butter if needed)
unsalted butter.
lemon juice.
almond extract.
all-purpose flour.

The crust is a classic pie dough made with all-purpose flour, cream cheese, and butter. The filling consists of sweet cherries and strawberries tossed in granulated sugar, almond extract, and lemon juice. You can use either fresh or frozen cherries for the pie filling; if using sour cherries, be sure to reduce the sugar accordingly. Once the pie is prepped, it's ready to bake! Bake at 375°F for 40-50 minutes or until the crust is golden brown and the filling is bubbling. Let cool before slicing and serving for a delicious finish to any meal!

Apple And Ginger Crumble Pie

Ingredients

1kg Granny Smith apples, peeled, cored, sliced.
Juice of 1 lemon.
1/3 cup (75g) caster sugar.
2 pieces stem ginger in syrup, finely chopped, plus 1 tbs syrup.
2 tbs plain flour.
Vanilla ice cream, to serve.

To make the apple and ginger crumble pie, preheat the oven to 190°C. In a large bowl, combine the sliced apples with lemon juice, caster sugar, chopped stem ginger and syrup, plain flour and a pinch of salt. Mix until all ingredients are thoroughly combined. Transfer the mixture into an 18x28cm baking dish lined with baking paper.

For the crumble topping, mix together 1 cup of plain flour and 50g melted butter until a crumbly texture forms. Sprinkle the mixture over the apple filling evenly, then bake in preheated oven for 35 minutes or until golden brown. Cool before serving with a scoop of vanilla ice cream. Enjoy!

Chocolate Hazelnut Tart

Ingredients
1 ½ cups graham cracker crumbs.
6 tablespoons salted butter, melted, (¾ of a stick)
¼ teaspoon salt.
1 cup hazelnuts plus 2 tablespoons, coarsely chopped.
1 cup heavy cream.
10 ½ oz fine-quality bittersweet chocolate chips, not unsweetened.
½ cup chocolate-hazelnut spread such as Nutella.

To make the tart crust, preheat the oven to 350°F. In a medium bowl, mix together the graham cracker crumbs, melted butter, and salt until combined. Press this mixture into an 8-inch tart pan with a removable bottom. Bake for 8 minutes or until golden in color. Remove from the oven and cool for about 10 minutes. Sprinkle the chopped hazelnuts on top of the cooled crust, pressing them lightly into it.

In a medium saucepan over low heat, heat the heavy cream until it begins to steam and bubbles start to form around the edges. Remove from the heat and add the bittersweet chocolate chips; stir gently until all of the chips are melted and the mixture is smooth. Pour this over the hazelnuts in the tart pan and spread it evenly with a rubber spatula.

In a separate medium bowl, mix together the remaining 2 tablespoons of chopped hazelnuts with ½ cup of chocolate-hazelnut spread until combined. Spoon this mixture on top of the chocolate-cream mixture in the tart pan, using a rubber spatula to spread it evenly. Place in the refrigerator for at least 2 hours before serving. Enjoy!

Crumble Cake With Berry

First make the crumble topping: Mix oats, flour, brown sugar, pecans, and salt in a medium bowl. ... Then make cake, preheat oven to 350 °F. ... Whisk baking powder, salt, and flour in a bowl. ... Mix blueberries, raspberries and half of crumble topping in a large bowl; sprinkle mixture over batter.

Next, prepare the crumble cake. Grease a 9" round baking pan with butter. Pour the cake batter into the greased pan and spread evenly. Sprinkle the berry mixture over the top of the batter, followed by ½ cup of remaining crumble topping. Bake for 30 minutes or until golden brown and a toothpick inserted into center of cake comes out clean. Let the crumble cake cool before serving. Enjoy!

Gingerbread Brownies

To prepare gingerbread brownies, begin by preheating the oven to 350 degrees Fahrenheit. Then combine all purpose flour, baking soda, salt, ground cinnamon, ground ginger and ground cloves in a medium bowl. Mix together until evenly combined and set aside. In another bowl, mix together unsweetened cocoa powder with melted unsalted butter. Beat until the mixture is smooth. Next, mix the dry ingredients with cocoa powder and butter mixture until just combined. Pour the batter into a greased 8x8 inch baking pan and spread evenly. Bake for 25-30 minutes or until an inserted toothpick comes out clean. Allow to cool before cutting into bars. Enjoy!

Oreo And Peanut Butter Pie

Ingredients
20 Oreos (or other chocolate cream biscuits)
175g unsalted butter.
400g crunchy peanut butter.
175g icing sugar, sifted.
200g good-quality dark chocolate, chopped.

These delicious Oreo and Peanut Butter Bars are super easy to prepare. First, line a 20x20cm square tin with baking parchment. Place the oreos in a food processor and blitz until they turn into fine crumbs. Alternatively, place the biscuits in a sealed plastic bag and crush them with a rolling pin.

In a medium saucepan, melt the butter over low heat. Once melted, stir in the peanut butter and icing sugar until fully incorporated.

Spoon this mixture into the tin, spreading it out evenly. Top with the Oreo crumbs and use a spoon to press them down gently into the mixture.

Melt the dark chocolate in a heatproof bowl set over a pan of simmering water, stirring until smooth. Pour the melted chocolate on top of the Oreo layer and spread it out evenly with a spoon or spatula.

Refrigerate for at least 2 hours before cutting into bars - the longer the better. Enjoy!

Store in an airtight container in the fridge for up to 5 days. These bars are perfect for a snack or even as dessert! Enjoy!

Spiced Pumpkin Pie

Ingredients

450g peeled butternut pumpkin, cut into 2cm pieces.
1 tbsp honey.
1 tbsp treacle or golden syrup.
1/3 firmly packed cup (80g) brown sugar.
1 tsp ground cinnamon, plus extra to serve.
1/2 tsp ground nutmeg.
1/2 tsp ground cloves.
1/2 tsp ground ginger.

To prepare the spiced pumpkin pie, start by pre-heating your oven to 200°C. Next, take a large baking tray and spread over it the butternut pumpkin pieces with some oil or butter. Place in the oven and roast for 15 minutes until lightly golden.

Once roasted, combine the pumpkin with honey, treacle or golden syrup and brown sugar in a large bowl. Add the ground cinnamon, nutmeg, cloves and ginger and mix until combined.

Next, take a greased 9 inch pie dish and pour in the spiced pumpkin mixture. Bake the pie in the pre-heated oven for 30 minutes or until lightly golden on top. Serve with extra ground cinnamon and a scoop of your favourite ice cream. Enjoy!

The spiced pumpkin pie is sure to be a delicious hit at any gathering or family dinner! With just 15 simple ingredients, the dish is easy to prepare and the perfect way to get into the spirit of fall. Get creative with how you serve the pie and enjoy!

Happy baking!

Panettone Bread

Ingredients

4 tbsp warm milk.
1 x 7g sachet fast-action dried yeast.
150g caster sugar.
250g butter, softened.
5 medium eggs, lightly beaten.
2 tsp vanilla extract.
grated zest of 1 lemon.
grated zest of 1 orange.

Making panettone bread is easy with the right ingredients and a few simple steps. To begin, combine the warm milk and dried yeast in a small bowl and mix until combined. In a separate large bowl, cream together the butter and sugar until light and fluffy. Slowly add eggs to the mixture one at a time, stirring well after each addition. Stir in the vanilla extract, lemon and orange zest. Add the milk and yeast mixture to the bowl and stir until combined.

Gradually add the panettone bread flour and mix on a low speed or by hand, until all of the ingredients are blended together. The dough should be soft but not sticky. Knead for 5 to 10 minutes, or until the dough is elastic and smooth. Place in a greased bowl and cover loosely with plastic wrap. Allow the dough to rise for about 2 hours, or until doubled in size.
Once risen, divide the dough into two pieces and shape each piece into a round loaf. Place the loaves onto baking trays lined with parchment paper and cover loosely again with plastic wrap. Allow the dough to rise for a further 1 hour, or until doubled in size again.

Preheat oven to 350F/180C and bake for 25 minutes, or until golden brown. Remove from the oven and allow to cool completely before serving. Enjoy your freshly made panettone bread!
Making this delicious Italian-style bread is now a cinch with these easy instructions. Who knew such an impressive loaf of bread could come together so quickly and easily? Try out this recipe today and see how it turns out for yourself! Bon appetite!

Cherry Tiramisu

100 ml coffee, unsweetened.
100 g dark chocolate (60% - 70% cacao)
100 g ladyfingers (biscuits)
3 eggs, free range.
500 g mascarpone cheese.
1 lemon, zest and juice.
3 tbsp Vin Santo or any other dessert wine.
170 g sugar.

To prepare the Cherry Tiramisu, begin by brewing 100 ml of strong coffee and setting it aside to cool. In a double boiler, melt the dark chocolate on low heat. Dip each ladyfinger biscuit in the warm melted chocolate and place them on a baking sheet lined with parchment paper. Place in refrigerator until the chocolate is set.

Separately, beat the eggs and sugar together until they become pale yellow in color. Add the mascarpone cheese to this mixture and mix until combined. Squeeze fresh lemon juice into the mixture, then add the zest of 1 lemon and 3 tablespoons of Vin Santo or other dessert wine.

Take a 6-inch springform pan and begin layering the ingredients. Begin by laying a layer of ladyfinger biscuits on the bottom of the pan, then spread half of the mascarpone mixture over top. Place another layer of chocolate-dipped ladyfingers over the mascarpone mixture, followed by another layer of mascarpone mixture and finally, a top layer of ladyfingers. Drizzle the remaining coffee on the top layer, then cover and place in refrigerator for 4-6 hours before serving.

When ready to serve, remove from springform pan and garnish with fresh cherries or any other desired topping. Enjoy!

Peach Pie

Ingredients

2/3 cup sugar.
1/3 cup Gold Medal™ All-Purpose Flour.
1/4 teaspoon ground cinnamon.
5 to 5 1/2 cups sliced peeled fresh peaches (5 to 6 medium)
1 teaspoon lemon juice.
1 package (12 oz) frozen Pillsbury™ Deep Dish Pie Crusts (2 Count)

To begin preparing your peach pie, preheat the oven to 425°F. Start by stirring together the sugar, flour and cinnamon in a large bowl until combined. Then, add the fresh peaches and lemon juice to the mixture and stir until everything is evenly coated.

Next, unroll one of the Pillsbury™ Deep Dish Pie Crusts and place it in a 9-inch deep dish pie plate. Pour the peaches into the pie crust and spread them evenly. Unroll the second crust and place it on top, sealing the edges with a fork and cutting slits to vent.

Finally, bake your peach pie for 40 minutes or until golden brown. Let the pie cool on a wire rack for about 10 minutes before serving. Enjoy!

Enjoying a freshly-baked peach pie is one of summer's greatest pleasures - follow these simple steps and you'll be able to enjoy your own tasty creation in no time! With a few basic ingredients, including sugar, Gold Medal™ All-Purpose Flour, cinnamon, fresh peaches and Pillsbury™ Deep Dish Pie Crusts, you'll have a delicious dessert to enjoy before you know it.

So don't wait - get baking today for an unforgettable summer treat! With this how-to guide, creating a classic peach pie has never been easier. Bon appétit!

Black Forest Tart

375g pack sweet shortcrust pastry, roughly chopped.
4 tbsp cocoa powder.
1 tsp vanilla extract.
50g plain flour, plus extra for dusting.
3 large eggs, 1 separated.
75g dark chocolate, broken up.
75g milk chocolate, broken up.
50g butter, diced.

To make the black forest tart, begin by preheating the oven to 190°C. Line a 20cm round tin with baking paper and grease it lightly. Place the pastry in a food processor and blend until it forms crumbs. Combine cocoa powder, vanilla extract and flour in a bowl and stir until combined. Add the eggs (except for the separated one) and mix until a dough forms.

Roll out the pastry on a floured surface and place it in the prepared tin, pressing around the edges. Prick lightly with a fork and bake in preheated oven for 15 minutes. Remove from oven and allow to cool slightly before brushing over with beaten egg white.

Combine the chocolate and butter in a bowl over a pan of simmering water. Stir until melted and combined, then spread over pastry base. Bake for another 25 minutes until set. Allow to cool completely before serving. Enjoy your black forest tart!

Enjoy your black forest tart! !!! The perfect treat for a special occasion.

To make the tart even more decadent, why not top it with some fresh cherries, whipped cream and dark chocolate shavings! Enjoy your black forest tart! !!! The perfect treat for any special occasion. !! :)

I want to take a moment to express my heartfelt gratitude for your recent purchase of my recipe book. As a passionate food lover, nothing makes me happier than sharing my favorite recipes with others. Your decision to invest in my book not only supports my dream, but also shows your commitment to expanding your culinary horizons.

I sincerely hope that the recipes in the book will inspire you to try new things and add some excitement to your meals.

Thank you again for your support and for being a part of this journey with me. I hope my book will bring you many happy and delicious moments in the kitchen.

www.ingramcontent.com/pod-product-compliance
Lightning Source LLC
Chambersburg PA
CBHW041151110526
44590CB00027B/4188